Pebble® Plus

Cool Robots
ROBOTS IN SPACE

by Kathryn Clay

Consulting Editor: Gail Saunders-Smith, PhD

Consultant: Seth Hutchinson, PhD
Department of Electrical and Computer Engineering
University of Illinois

CAPSTONE PRESS
a capstone imprint

Pebble Plus is published by Capstone Press,
1710 Roe Crest Drive, North Mankato, Minnesota 56003
www.capstonepub.com

Library of Congress Cataloging-in-Publication Data
Clay, Kathryn, author.
 Robots in space / Kathryn Clay.
    pages cm.—(Pebble plus) (Cool robots)
 Summary: "Simple text and full-color photographs describe eight different space robots and the work these robots do."—Provided by publisher.
 Includes bibliographical references and index.
 ISBN 978-1-4914-0585-7 (hb)—ISBN 978-1-4914-0649-6 (pb)—ISBN 978-1-4914-0619-9 (eb)
1. Space robotics—Juvenile literature. 2. Robots—Juvenile literature. 3. Space probes—Juvenile literature. 4. Outer space—Exploration—Juvenile literature. I. Title.
 TJ211.2.C554 2015
 629.43—dc23   2014002418

Editorial Credits
Erika L. Shores, editor; Terri Poburka, designer; Katy LaVigne, production specialist

Photo Credits
NASA, 7, 9, 15, 21, JHU/APL, 11, JPL, 19, JPL-Caltech, cover, 5, 13, JPL-Caltech/MSSS, 17

Design Elements
Shutterstock: Irena Peziene, Kate Pru

Note to Parents and Teachers

The Cool Robots set supports national science standards related to science, technology, engineering, and mathematics. This book describes and illustrates space robots. The images support early readers in understanding the text. The repetition of words and phrases helps early readers learn new words. This book also introduces early readers to subject-specific vocabulary words, which are defined in the Glossary section. Early readers may need assistance to read some words and to use the Table of Contents, Glossary, Read More, Internet Sites, and Index sections of the book.

Printed in China
032014   008085LEOF14

Table of Contents

Working in Space

Robots often work in places
too dangerous for humans.
People use robots to learn
about outer space.

Scientists set up an area similar to land on Mars. They use the area to drive test rovers.

Hands and Arms

Together NASA and
General Motors made
a robotic glove. The glove
helps astronauts better
grip tools.

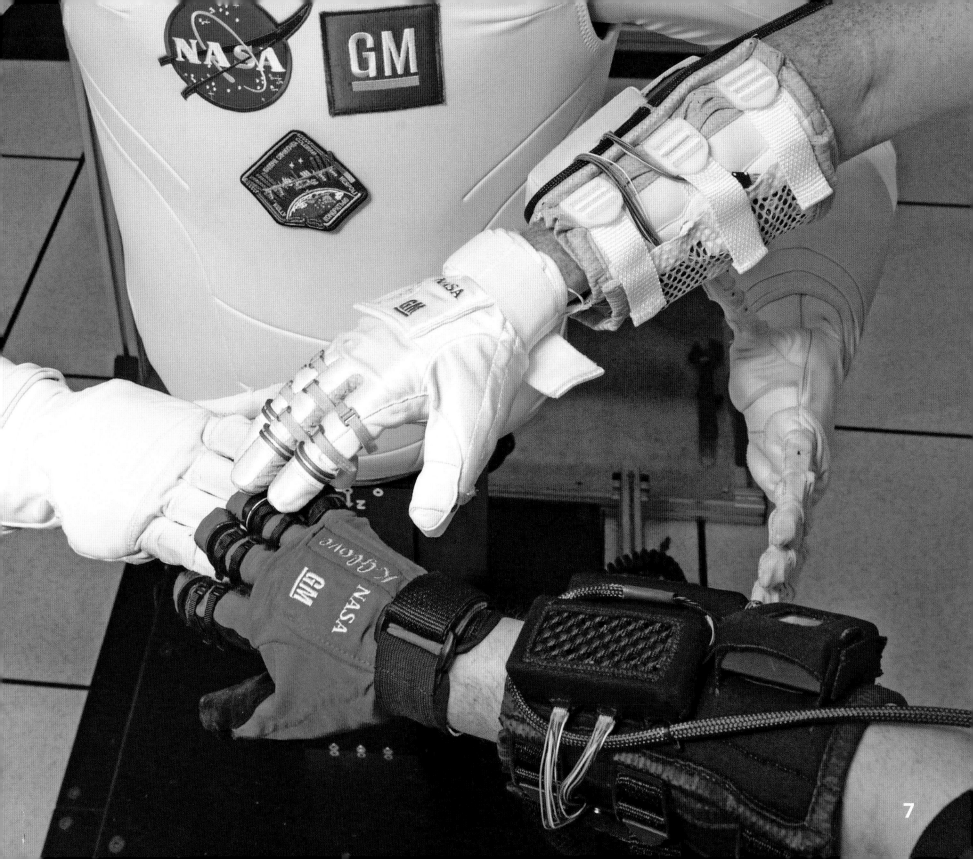

Canadarm2 is no small robot. Astronauts control the nearly 60-foot (18-meter) arm from inside the *International Space Station.*

Explorers

Unmanned probes fly through space.
The *Van Allen* probes send back
information about the Sun.

Voyager 2 has travelled through space for more than 35 years. It has sent back pictures of Neptune, Uranus, and other objects in deep space.

Rovers study planets.

Spirit and *Opportunity* landed on Mars in 2004. The robots explored the rocky, red planet.

The *Curiosity* rover landed
on Mars in 2012.
Its robotic arm has a scoop
that gathers soil from Mars.

Future Space Robots

Groups of spider-bots might explore planets in the future. Tiny legs move the robots quickly across rough ground.

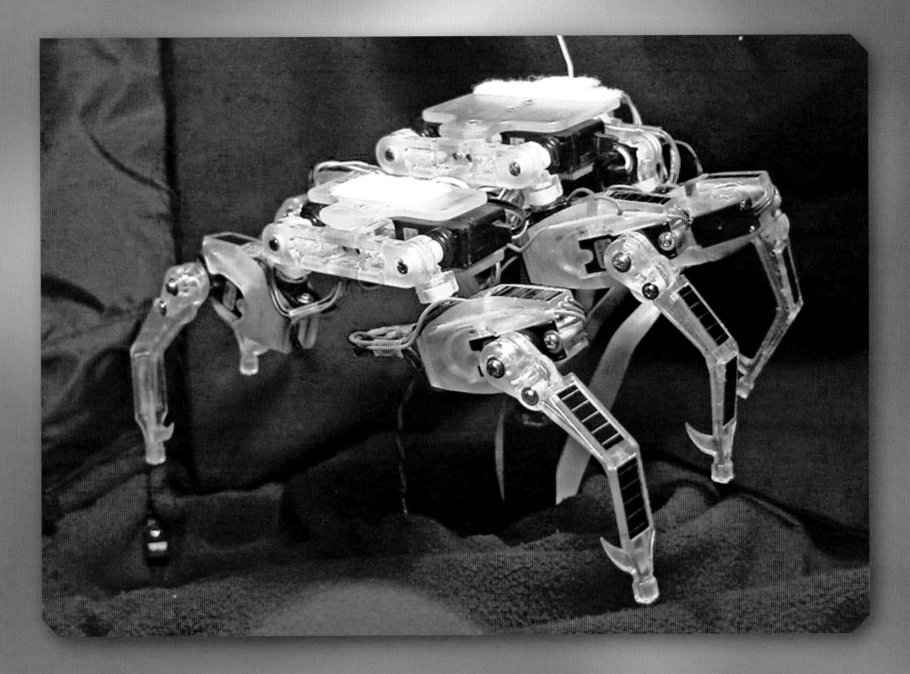

Today Robonaut 2 works inside the space station. One day the humanlike robot might go to the moon or even Mars.

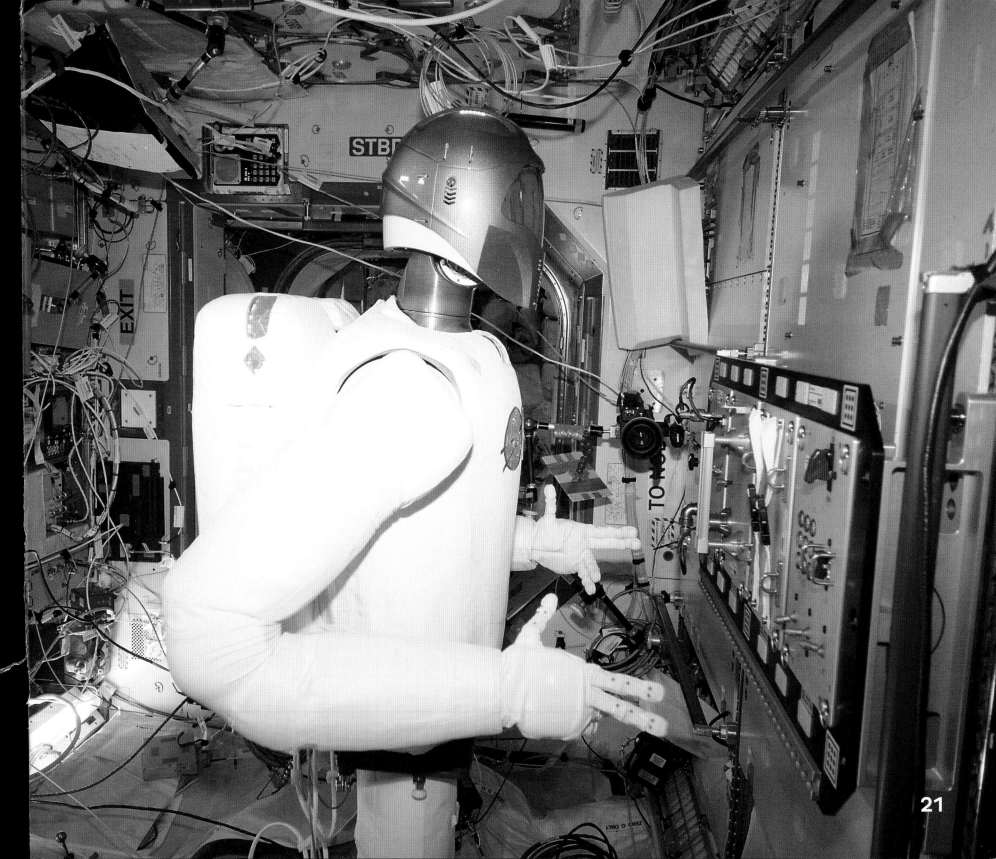

Glossary

astronaut—a person who is trained to live and work in space

NASA—National Aeronautics and Space Administration

planet—a large object that moves around a star

probe—a small vehicle used to explore objects in outer space

robonaut—a robot that looks like a human astronaut

robot—a machine that can do work and is operated by remote control or a computer

rover—a small vehicle that people can move by using remote control

space station—a spacecraft that circles Earth in which astronauts can live for long periods of time

unmanned—drives or flies without a person onboard

Read More

Furstinger, Nancy. *Robots in Space.* Robots Everywhere! Minneapolis: Lerner Publications Company, 2015.

Rustad, Martha E. H. *Space Vehicles.* Exploring Space. Mankato, Minn.: Capstone Press, 2012.

Internet Sites

FactHound offers a safe, fun way to find Internet sites related to this book. All of the sites on FactHound have been researched by our staff.

Here's all you do:

Visit *www.facthound.com*

Type in this code: 9781491405857

Super-cool stuff!

Check out projects, games and lots more at
www.capstonekids.com

Critical Thinking Using the Common Core

1. Look at the photo on page 18. Why is spider-bot a good name for this robot? (Integration of Knowledge and Details)

2. Think about what you know about outer space. What are some reasons scientists send robots into space rather than humans? (Integration of Knowledge and Details)

Index

Word Count: 167

Grade: 1

Early-Intervention Level: 20